HIPPOCRENE

Hindi
Children's
Picture Dictionary

English – Hindi
Hindi – English

HIPPOCRENE BOOKS
NEW YORK, NY

Text and illustrations © 2006 Hippocrene Books, Inc.

ISBN 0-7818-1129-5

Publisher: George Blagowidow
Series Editor: Robert Stanley Martin
Interior illustrations: Nicholas Voltaggio
English word list: Priti Gress, Robert Stanley Martin
Hindi translation and pronunciation material: Todd Scudiere
Hindi copyeditor: Susham Bedi
Main cover illustration: Robert Stanley Martin; colors by Cynthia Mallard, Cynergie Studio, Raleigh, NC
Inset cover illustrations: Nicholas Voltaggio

Book and series design: www.GoCreativeDesign.com
Additional design, typesetting, and pre-press production: Susan Ahlquist, Perfect Setting, East Hampton, NY

For information, address:

Hippocrene Books, Inc.
171 Madison Avenue
New York, NY 10016
www.hippocrenebooks.com

Cataloging-in-Publication data available from the Library of Congress

Printed in China.

TABLE OF CONTENTS

Letter (s)	Pronunciation

Vowels

अ · **a,** like the *u* in the English "b**u**s"

आ · **aa,** like *a* in the English "f**a**ther"

इ,ई · **i,** like *i* in the English "p**i**n"

· **ee,** like *ee* in the English "sl**ee**ve"

उ ऊ · **u,** like *u* in the English "p**u**t"

· **uu,** like *oo* in the English "f**oo**l"

ए,ऐ · **ay,** like *a* in the English "g**a**me" or "c**a**ke"

· **ai,** like *e* as in the English "m**e**n" and for some speakers in different regions, **i** like *i* in the English "sm**i**le"

ओ · **o,** like *o* in the English "m**o**st"

औ · **au,** like *o* in the English "**o**range" or sometimes stronger like *ou* in the English "c**ou**ch"

Consonants

क · **ka,** like *k* in the English "s**k**irt"

ख · **kha,** like *kh* in the English "**kh**aki"

ग · **ga,** like *g* in the English "sprin**g**"

घ · **gha,** like *g* in the English "**g**um"

च · **cha,** like *ch* in the English "ri**ch**" or the final *ch* sound in "chur**ch**"

छ · **Cha,** like *ch* in the English "**ch**arm" or the initial *ch* sound in "**ch**urch"

ज · **ja,** like *ge* in the English "brid**ge**"

झ · **jha,** like *j* in the English "**j**ump"

ञ · **jna,** like *n* in the English "i**n**jury"

ट · **Ta,** like *t* in the English "plan**t**"

ठ · **Tha,** like *t* in the English "**t**able"

ड · **Da,** like *d* in the English "blan**d**"

ढ · **Dha,** like *d* in the English "**d**am"

द · **da,** like *d* in the French "Concor**d**e"

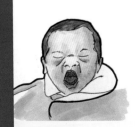

Letter (s)	Pronunciation
ड़	**Ra**. To make this sound, place the tip of your tongue on the roof of your mouth and say "da," flapping the tip of your tongue slightly.
ढ़	**Rha**, same as above letter, but aspirated as well. Follow the above instructions for **Ra**, and this time exhale slightly.
ण	**Na**, like *n* in the English "**n**ine"
त	**ta**, like *t* in the French "ver**t**c"
थ	**tha**, like *t* in the English "**t**alk"
द	**da**, like *d* in the French "Concor**d**e"
ध	**dha**, like *d* in the English "**d**onut"
न	**na**, like *n* in the English "bea**n**"
प	**pa**, like *p* in the English "cu**p**"
फ	**pha**, like *ph* in the English "**p**arty"
ब	**ba**, like *b* in the English "la**b**"
भ	**bha**, like *b* in the English "**b**akery"
म	**ma**, like *m* in the English "**m**other"
य	**ya**, like *y* in the English "**y**ard"
र	**ra**, like *r* in the English "**r**ap" but rolled or trilled slightly.
ल	**la**, like *l* in the English "**l**ove"
व	**va**, like *v* in the English "lo**v**e" and sometimes like *w* in the English "**w**ater"
श	**sha**, like *sh* in the English "ca**sh**" or "**sh**opping"
ष	**Sha**, like *sh* in the English "ca**sh**"
स	**sa**, like *s* in the English "**s**oap"
ह	**ha**, like *h* in the English "**h**ouse"

Perso-Arabic Sounds

फ़	**fa**, like *f* in the English "**f**ake"
ज़	**za**, like *z* in the English "**z**ebra"
क़	**qa**, like *k* in the English "s**k**irt" but said in the back of the throat.
ख़	**qha**; same as **kha**, but said in the back of the throat.
ग़	**qga**; same as *g* in the English son**g**, but said in the back of the throat.

Note on the Pronunciation of Words

In this text, nasalized vowel sounds will be transliterated as ñ. This is not to be pronounced as a hard "n" sound. For example, say the English word "hay" aloud. Now, holding your nose closed, say it again. The sound you are now hearing would be represented by "hayñ."

Aspirated sounds require you to breathe out a little when you say them. In this book, whenever you see an "h" immediately after a consonant, you will know that the word requires you to do this.

Retroflex sounds, represented in this book by capitalized letters such as **Da** and **Ta** are formed by placing the tip of the tongue on the roof of the mouth. For instance, with the **Ta** sound, place the tip of your tongue on the roof of your mouth and say **Ta**. For a sound that is both retroflex and aspirated, such as **Tha**, follow the same instructions but this time exhale slightly to produce a "ha" sound after the consonant.

This transliteration scheme has been followed in the text, with some exceptions. In some cases slight substitutions were made in order to provide the reader with a more common pronunciation.

afraid डरा हुआ
Da-raa hu-aa

airplane हवाई जहाज़
ha-vaa-ee ja-haaz

alphabet वर्णमाला
var-Na-maa-laa

ambulance अस्पताल गाड़ी
as-pa-taal gaa-Ree

angry नाराज़
naa-raaz

ant चींटी
chiñ-Tee

a b c d e f g h i j k l m n o p q r s t u v w x y z

apartment   फ़्लैट
                                  flaiT

apple   सेब
                                  sayb

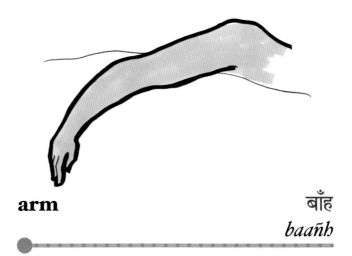

arm   बाँह
                                  baañh

autumn   पतझड़
                                  pat-jhaR

a b c d e f g h i j k l m n o p q r s t u v w x y z

baby बच्चा
bacchaa

ball गेंद
gaynd

balloon गुब्बारा
gubb-aa-raa

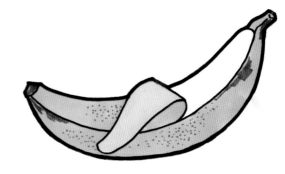

banana केला
kay-laa

bank बैंक
baiṅk

barrel पीपा
pee-paa

a b c d e f g h i j k l m n o p q r s t u v w x y z

baseball बेसबॉल
bays-baal

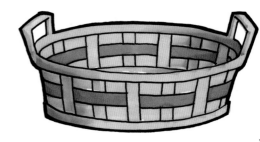

basket टोकरी
To-ka-ree

bat बैट
baiT

bathroom गुसलख़ाना
gu-sal-qhaa-naa

bathtub स्नान का टब
snaan kaa Tab

beach समुद्र तट
sa-mu-dra Tat

a b c d e f g h i j k l m n o p q r s t u v w x y z

beans सेम
saym

bear भालू
bhaa-luu

bed बिस्तर
bis-tar

bedroom सोने का कमरा
sonay kaa kam-raa

bee मधुमक्खी
ma-dhu-makkhee

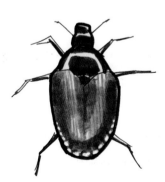

beetle भौंरा
bhauñ-raa

a b c d e f g h i j k l m n o p q r s t u v w x y z

Bb

bell घंटा
ghan-Taa

bellybutton नाभि
naa-bhi

belt पेटी
pay-Tee

bench बेंच
bayñch

bicycle साइकिल
saai-kil

big बड़ा
ba-Raa

a b c d e f g h i j k l m n o p q r s t u v w x y z

Bb

binoculars　दूरबीन
duur-been

bird　चिड़िया
chi-Ri-yaa

birthday　जन्मदिन
ja-nam din

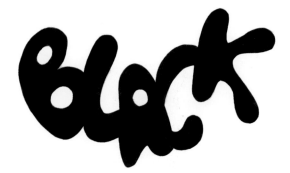

black　काला
kaa-laa

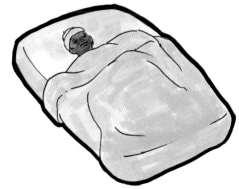

blanket　कंबल
kam-bal

blinds　चिक्
chiq

a b c d e f g h i j k l m n o p q r s t u v w x y z

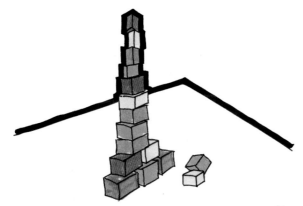

blocks ब्लॉक्स
blaaks

blue नीला
nee-laa

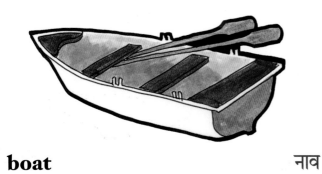

boat नाव
naav

book किताब
ki-taab

bottle बोतल
bo-tal

bowl कटोरा
ka-To-raa

a b c d e f g h i j k l m n o p q r s t u v w x y z

box डिब्बा
Dibbaa

boy लड़का
laR-kaa

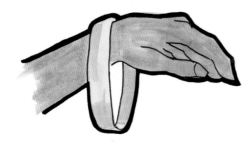

bracelet कंगन
kan-gan

bread रोटी
ro-Tee

breakfast नाश्ता
naash-taa

bridge पुल
pul

a b c d e f g h i j k l m n o p q r s t u v w x y z

broom   झाड़ू
jhaa-Ruu

brown   भूरा
bhuu-raa

brush   ब्रश
brash

bucket   बाल्टी
baal-Tee

a b c d e f g h i j k l m n o p q r s t u v w x y z

building   इमारत
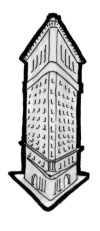
i-maa-rat

bus   बस

bas

butter   मक्खन
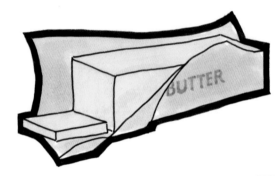
makkhan

butterfly   तितली

ti-ta-lee

(to) buy   खरीदना

kha-reed-naa

a b **c** d e f g h i j k l m n o p q r s t u v w x y z

cabinet अलमारी
al-maa-ree

cake केक
kek

calendar कैलेंडर
kai-len-Dar

camel ऊँट
uuñT

camera कैमरा
kai-ma-raa

candle मोमबत्ती
mom-battee

a b c d e f g h i j k l m n o p q r s t u v w x y z

Cc

candy मिठाई
mi-Thaa-ee

car गाड़ी
gaa-Ree

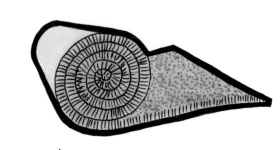

carpet दरी
da-ree

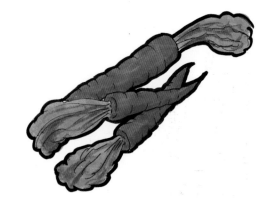

carrot गाजर
gaa-jar

(to) carry ढोना
Dho-naa

castle क़िला
qi-laa

a b c d e f g h i j k l m n o p q r s t u v w x y z

cat बिल्ली
billee

caterpillar इल्ली
illee

cave गुफ़ा
gu-faa

ceiling छत
Chat

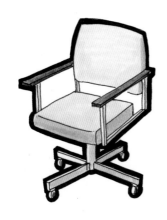

chair कुर्सी
kur-see

cheek गाल
gaal

a b c d e f g h i j k l m n o p q r s t u v w x y z

Cc

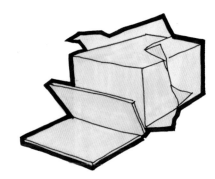

cheese पनीर
pa-neer

chef रसोइया
ra-soi-yaa

cherry चेरी
chay-ree

chest पेटी
pay-Tee

chicken मुर्गी
mur-gee

child बच्चा
bacchaa

a b c d e f g h i j k l m n o p q r s t u v w x y z

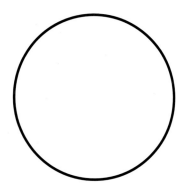

circle गोला
go-laa

circus सरकस
sar-kas

city शहर
sha-har

(to) climb चढ़ना
chaRh-naa

clock घड़ी
gha-Ree

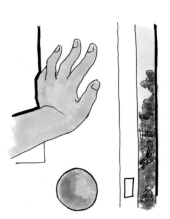

(to) close बन्द करना
band kar-naa

a b c d e f g h i j k l m n o p q r s t u v w x y z

Cc

closet   अलमारी
al-maa-ree

cloud   बादल
baa-dal

clown   विदूषक
vi-duu-Shak

coat   कोट
koT

coffee   कौफ़ी
kau-fee

cold   ठण्डा
ThaN-Daa

a b c d e f g h i j k l m n o p q r s t u v w x y z

comb कंघी
kan-Ghee

computer कंप्यूटर
kam-pyuu-Tar

construction worker मज़दूर
maz-duur

(to) cook पकाना
pa-kaa-naa

cookie मीठा बिस्कुट
mee-Thaa bis-kuT

corn मक्का
makkaa

a b c d e f g h i j k l m n o p q r s t u v w x y z

cracker बिस्कुट
bis-kuT

(to) crawl रेंगना
rayṅg-naa

crayon चित्रांकनी
chi-traan-ka-nee

crib खटोला
kha-To-laa

crocodile मगर
magar

(to) cry रोना
ro-naa

curtain परदा
par-daa

a b c d e f g h i j k l m n o p q r s t u v w x y z

Dd

(to) dance   नाचना
naach-naa

deer   हिरन
hi-ran

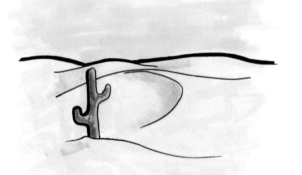

desert   रेगिस्तान
ray-gi-staan

desk   डेस्क
Daysk

dessert   मिठाई
mi-Thaa-ee

diamond   हीरा
hee-raa

a b c **d** e f **g** h i j **k** l **m** n o p q r s t u v w x y **z**

dinner रात का खाना
raat kaa khaa-naa

dinosaur डाइनसॉर
Daai-na-saar

dirty गंदा
gan-daa

doctor डॉक्टर
Daak-Tar

dog कुत्ता
kuttaa

doll गुड़िया
gu-Ri-yaa

a b c **d** e f g h i j k l m n o p q r s t u v w x y z

Dd

dolphin डॉलफ़िन
Daal-fin

donkey गधा
ga-dhaa

door दरवाज़ा
dar-vaa-zaa

down नीचे
nee-chay

downstairs नीचे
nee-chay

dragon ड्रैगन
Drai-gan

a b c d e f g h i j k l m n o p q r s t u v w x y z

drawer
दराज़
da-raaz

dress
ड्रैस
Drais

(to) drink
पीना
pee-naa

drum
ढोल
Dhol

duck
बतख़
ba-taqh

a b c **d** e f g h i j k l m n o p q r s t u v w x y z

Ee

eagle उकाब
u-kaab

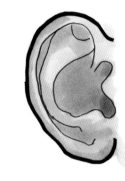

ear कान
kaan

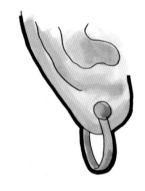

earring बालियाँ
baa-li-yaań

(to) eat खाना
Khaa-naa

egg अण्डा
aN-Daa

a b c d **e** f g h i j k l m n o p q r s t u v w x y z

eight　　आठ
aaTh

elephant　　हाथी
haa-thee

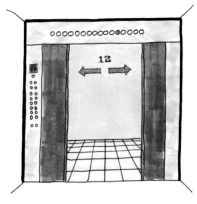

elevator　　लिफ़्ट
lifT

empty　　ख़ाली
qhaa-lee

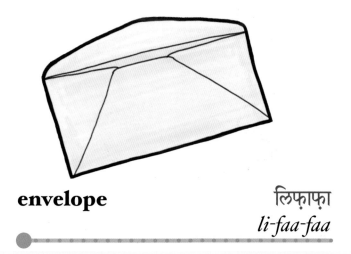

envelope　　लिफ़ाफ़ा
li-faa-faa

a b c d **e** f g h i j k l m n o p q r s t u v w x y z

Ee

escalator   चलती सीढ़ी
chal-tee see-Rhee

evening   शाम
shaam

eye   आँख
aañkh

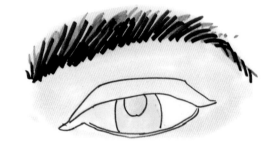

eyebrow   भौंह
bhauñh

eyeglasses   चश्मा
chash-maa

a b c d **e** f g h i j k l m n o p q r s t u v w x y z

Ff

face   चेहरा
che-ha-raa

family   परिवार
pa-ri-vaar

fan   पंखा
pan-Khaa

feather   पर
par

(to) feed   खिलाना
Khi-laa-naa

a b c d e **f** g h i j k l m n o p q r s t u v w x y z

fence बाड़
baaR

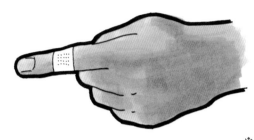

finger अँगुली
añ-gu-lee

fire आग
aag

fire engine दमकल
damkal

firefighter आग बुझाने वाला
aag bu-jhaane vaa-laa

fish मछली
maCh-lee

a b c d e **f** g h i j k l m n o p q r s t u v w x y z

five पाँच
paañch

flag झण्डा
jhaN-Daa

flashlight टॉर्च
Taarch

floor फ़र्श
farsh

flower फूल
phuul

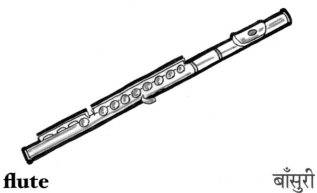

flute बाँसुरी
baañ-su-ree

a b c d e **f** g h i j k l m n o p q r s t u v w x y z

(to) fly उड़ना
uR-naa

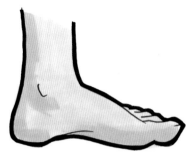

foot पैर
pair

forest वन
van

fork काँटा
kaañ-Taa

fountain फ़व्वारा
favvaa-raa

four चार
chaar

a b c d e **f** g h i j k l m n o p q r s t u v w x y z

fox लोमड़ी
lom-Ree

Friday शुक्रवार
shu-kra-vaar

friend दोस्त
dost

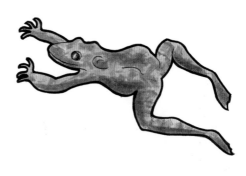

frog मेंढक
mayñ-Dhak

fruit फल
phal

full पूर्ण
puurN

a b c d e **f** g h i j k l m n o p q r s t u v w x y z

game खेल
khel

garden बाग़
baaqg

gasoline पेट्रोल
pe-Trol

gift उपहार
u-pa-haar

giraffe जिराफ़
ji-raaf

girl लड़की
laR-kee

a b c d e f **g** h i j k l m n o p q r s t u v w x y z

(to) give   देना
de-naa

glass   ग्लास
glaas

globe   ग्लोब
glob

golf   गॉल्फ़
gaalf

Good night.   शुभ रात्रि
shubh raa-tri

Good-bye.   नमस्ते
namastay

a b c d e f **g** h i j k l m n o p q r s t u v w x y z

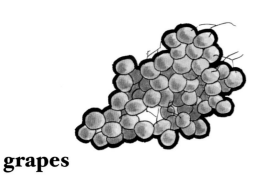

grapes अंगूर
an-guur

grasshopper टिड्डा
TiDDaa

green हरा
ha-raa

guitar गिटार
gi-Taar

gymnastics व्यायाम
vyaa-yaam

a b c d e f **g** h i j k l m n o p q r s t u v w x y z

hair बाल
baal

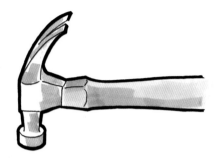

hammer हथौड़ा
ha-thau-Raa

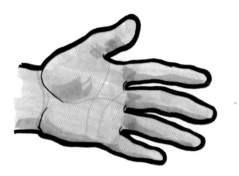

hand हाथ
haath

happy खुश
khush

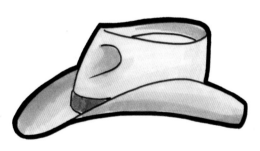

hat टोपी
To-pee

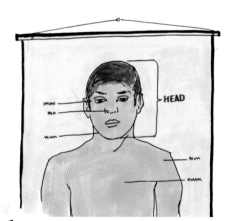

head सिर
sir

a b c d e f g **h** i j k l m n o p q r s t u v w x y z

heart दिल
dil

helicopter हेलिकापटर
helikaapTar

Hello. नमस्ते
namastay

(to) hide छिपाना
Chi-pa-naa

highway राजमार्ग
raaj-maarg

hippopotamus दरियाई घोड़ा
dari-yaaee gho-Raa

a b c d e f g **h** i j k l m n o p q r s t u v w x y z

horse　　　　　　　　धोड़ा
gho-Raa

hospital　　　　　　अस्पताल
as-pa-taal

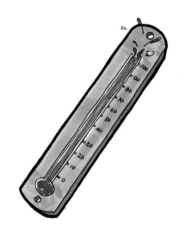

hot　　　　　　　　गरम
ga-ram

house　　　　　　मकान
ma-kaan

(to) hug　　　　गले लगाना
gale la-gaa-naa

a b c d e f g **h** i j k l m n o p q r s t u v w x y z

ice cream　　　　आइसक्रीम
aais-kreem

ice cube　　　　बर्फ़
barf

ice-skating　　बर्फ़ पर स्केटिंग करना
barf par skay-Ting kar-naa

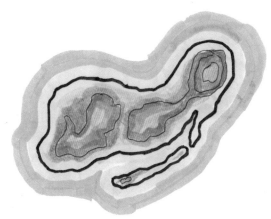

island　　　　टापू
Taa-puu

a b c d e f g h i j k l m n o p q r s t u v w x y z

jacket जाकेट
jaa-kayT

jam जैम
jaim

jar मर्तबान
marta-baan

jigsaw puzzle पहेली
pa-hay-lee

juice रस
ras

(to) jump कूदना
kuud-naa

jungle जंगल
jan-gal

a b c d e f g h i **j** k l m n o p q r s t u v w x y z

kangaroo कंगारू
kan-gaa-ruu

key चाबी
caa-bee

king राजा
raa-jaa

kiss चुम्मा
chummaa

kitchen रसोईघर
rasoee-ghar

a b c d e f g h i j **k** l m n o p q r s t u v w x y z

kite चील
cheel

kitten बिलौटा
bi-lau-Taa

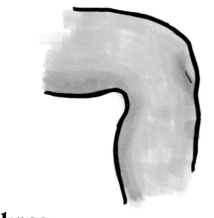

knee घुटना
ghuT-naa

knife चाकू
chaa-kuu

knot गाँठ
gaañTh

a b c d e f g h i j **k** l m n o p q r s t u v w x y z

ladder सीढ़ी
see-Rhee

ladybug बीर बहुटा
beer ba-hu-Taa

lamb मेमना
maym-naa

lamp लैंप
laimp

(to) laugh हँसना
hańs-naa

a b c d e f g h i j k **l** m n o p q r s t u v w x y z

leaf पत्ता
pattaa

leg टाँग
Taañg

lemon नीबू
nii-buu

library पुस्तकालय
pusta-kaa-lay

lion सिंह
siñha

a b c d e f g h i j k **l** m n o p q r s t u v w x y z

living room बैठक
bai-Thak

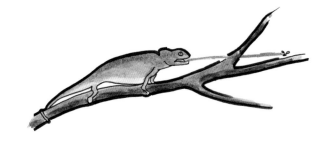

lizard छिपकली
Chip-ka-lee

lobster समुद्री झींगा
sa-mu-dree jheeń-gaa

loud तेज़
tez

lunch दिन का खाना
din kaa khaa-naa

a b c d e f g h i j k l m n o p q r s t u v w x y z

Mm

mail carrier
डाकिया
Daa-ki-yaa

mailbox
पोस्ट बॉक्स
posT baaks

man
आदमी
aad-mee

map
नक्शा
naq-shaa

mask
नकाब
na-kaab

medicine
दवा
da-vaa

a b c d e f g h i j k l **m** n o p q r s t u v w x y z

menu मेन्यू
may-nyuu

milk दूध
duudh

mirror दर्पण
darpaN

mitten दस्ताना
das-taa-naa

Monday सोमवार
som-vaar

a b c d e f g h i j k l **m** n o p q r s t u v w x y z

Mm

money पैसा
pai-saa

monkey बन्दर
bandar

moon चन्द्र
candra

morning सवेरा
sa-ve-raa

a b c d e f g h i j k l **m** n o p q r s t u v w x y z

mountain पहाड़
pa-haaR

mouse चुहिया
chu-hi-yaa

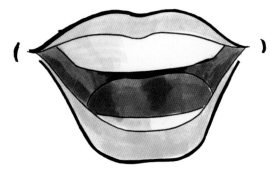

mouth मुँह
muñh

movie theater सिनेमा
si-nay-maa

museum संग्रहालय
san-gra-haa-lye

a b c d e f g h i j k l **m** n o p q r s t u v w x y z

nail कील
keel

name नाम
naam

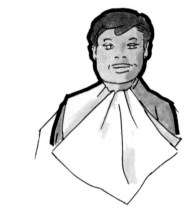

napkin नैपकिन
naip-kin

necklace हार
haar

neighborhood पड़ोस
pa-Ros

a b c d e f g h i j k l m n o p q r s t u v w x y z

nest   घोंसला
ghoñ-sa-laa

newspaper   समाचारपत्र
sa-maa-chaar patr

night   रात
raat

9

nine   नौ
nau

nurse   नर्स
nars

a b c d e f g h i j k l m **n** o p q r s t u v w x y z

ocean महासागर
ma-haa-saa-gar

old पुराना
pu-raa-naa

one एक
ek

(to) open खोलना
khol-naa

orange [color] नारंगी
naa-ran-gee

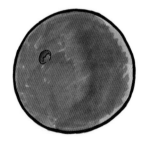

orange [fruit] सन्तरा
san-ta-raa

oven भट्टी
bhaTThee

a b c d e f g h i j k l m n o p q r s t u v w x y z

Pp

paint पेंट
painT

pajamas पाजामा
paa-jaa-maa

pants पतलून
pa-ta-luun

paper काग़ज़
kaa-gaz

park पार्क
paark

parking lot गाड़ी स्थान
gaa-Ree sthaan

a b c d e f g h i j k l m n o p q r s t u v w x y z

parrot तोता
to-taa

party पार्टी
paar-Tee

peach आड़ू
aaRuu

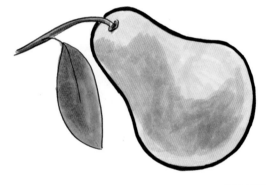

pear नाशपाती
naash-paa-tee

pen क़लम
qa-lam

pencil पेंसिल
payn-sil

a b c d e f g h i j k l m n o **p** q r s t u v w x y z

Pp

people लोग
lowg

pepper काली मिर्च
kaa-lee mirch

photograph फ़ोटो
fo-To

piano पियानो
pi-yaa-no

pie पाइ
paai

pig सूअर
suu-ar

a b c d e f g h i j k l m n o **p** q r s t u v w x y z

pillow तकिया
ta-ki-yaa

planet ग्रह
graha

(to) play खेलना
khayl-naa

pink गुलाबी
gu-laa-bee

plate प्लेट
playT

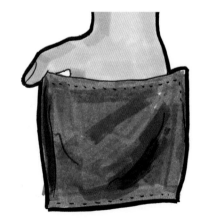

pocket जेब
jeb

a b c d e f g h i j k l m n o **p** q r s t u v w x y z

Pp

police officer

पुलिस
pu-lis

post office

डाक घर
Daak ghar

pot

हँडिया
hañ-Di-yaa

potato

आलू
aaluu

(to) pull

खींचना
kheeñch-naa

pumpkin

कददू
kadduu

a b c d e f g h i j k l m n o **p** q r s t u v w x y z

puppet पुतली
put-lee

puppy पिल्ला
pillaa

purple बैंगनी
baiñ-ga-nee

purse पर्स
pars

queen रानी
raa-nee

quiet शान्त
shaant

a b c d e f g h i j k l m n o **p** **q** r s t u v w x y z

rabbit　　　　　　　　ख़रगोश
qhar-gosh

radio　　　　　　　　रेडियो
ray-Di-yo

rain　　　　　　　　बारिश
baa-rish

rainbow　　　　　　इन्द्रधनुष
indra-dha-nuSh

(to) read　　　　　　पढ़ना
paRh-naa

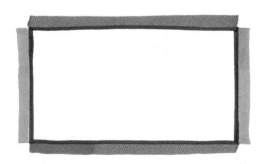

rectangle　　　　　　आयत
aa-yat

a b c d e f g h i j k l m n o p q **r** s t u v w x y z

red लाल
laal

refrigerator फ्रिज
frij

restaurant रेस्तराँ
ray-sta-raañ

rice चावल
caa-val

(to) ride सवारी करना
sa-vaa-ree kar-naa

ring अँगूठी
añ-guu-Thee

a b c d e f g h i j k l m n o p q r s t u v w x y z

river   नदी
na-dee

road   सड़क
sa-Rak

rock   चट्टान
chaTTaan

roof   छत
Chat

rooster   मुरगा
mur-gaa

rose   गुलाब
gu-laab

(to) run   दौड़ना
dauR-naa

a b c d e f g h i j k l m n o p q **r** s t u v w x y z

sad उदास
u-daas

salad सलाद
sa-laad

salt नमक
namak

sandal चप्पल
chap-pal

sandwich सैंडविच
sainD-vich

Saturday शनिवार
sha-ni-vaar

a b c d e f g h i j k l m n o p q r **s** t u v w x y z

saxophone   सैक्सोफ़ोन
saiks-o-fon

scarf   दुपट्टा
du-paTTaa

school   विद्यालय
vi-dyaa-lay

scissors   कैंची
kaiñ-chee

screwdriver   पेंचकश
paynch-kash

seesaw   झूमाझूमी
jhuu-maa-jhuu-mee

a b c d e f g h i j k l m n o p q r **s** t u v w x y z

seven सात
saat

shark हाँगर
haañ-gar

sheep भेड़
bhayR

shell सीप
seep

shirt कमीज़
ka-meez

shoe जूता
juu-taa

a b c d e f g h i j k l m n o p q r **s** t u v w x y z

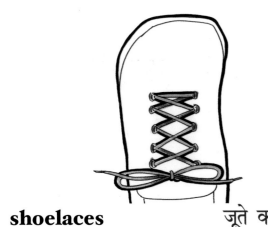

shoelaces   जूते का फ़ीता
juu-tay kaa fee-taa

short   छोटा
ChoTaa

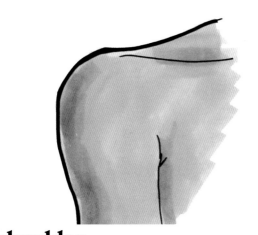

shoulder   कंधा
kan-dhaa

(to) shout   चिल्लाना
chillaa-naa

sick   बीमार
bee-maar

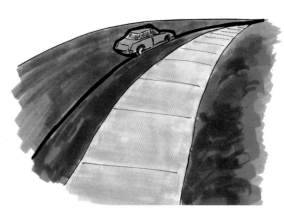

sidewalk   फुटपाथ
phuTh-paath

a b c d e f g h i j k l m n o p q r **s** t u v w x y z

(to) sing गाना
gaa-naa

sink हौज़
hauz

(to) sit बैठना
baiTh-naa

6

six छह
Chay

skiing स्कीइंग करना
skee-ing kar-naa

a b c d e f g h i j k l m n o p q r **s** t u v w x y z

Ss

skirt घाघरा
ghaa-gha-raa

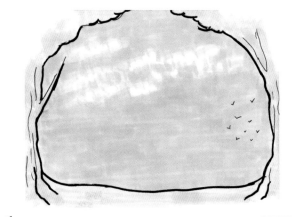

sky आकाश
aa-kaash

sled बर्फ़ गाड़ी
barf-gaaRee

(to) sleep सोना
so-naa

slide स्लाइड
slaaiD

small छोटा
Cho-Taa

a b c d e f g h i j k l m n o p q r s t u v w x y z

Ss

smile मुस्कराहट
mus-ka-raa-haT

smoke धुआँ
dhu-aañ

snake साँप
saañp

(to) sneeze छींकना
Cheenk-naa

snow बफ़
barf

soap साबुन
saabun

a b c d e f g h i j k l m n o p q r **s** t u v w x y z

soccer   फुटबाल
phuT-baal

sock   मोज़ा
mo-zaa

sofa   सोफ़ा
so-faa

soup   शोरबा
shor-baa

sour   खट्टा
khaTTaa

spider   मकड़ी
mak-Ree

a b c d e f g h i j k l m n o p q r s t u v w x y z

spoon चम्मच
cammach

spring वसंत
vasant

square चौकोर
chau-kor

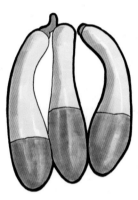

squash कुम्हड़ा
kum-ha-Raa

squirrel गिलहरी
gi-la-ha-ree

(to) stand खड़ा होना
kha-Raa ho-naa

a b c d e f g h i j k l m n o p q r s t u v w x y z

star   तारा
taa-raa

steps   क़दम
qa-dam

stomach   पेट
payT

strawberry   स्ट्राबेरी
sTraa-bay-ri

street   सड़क
sa-Rak

stroller   प्राम
praam

subway   भूमिगत रेलवे
bhuu-mi-gat rayl-vay

a b c d e f g h i j k l m n o p q r s t u v w x y z

sugar　　चीनी
chee-nee

suitcase　　सूटकेस
suuT-kays

summer　　गरमी
gar-mee

sun　　सूर्य
surya

Sunday　　रविवार
ra-vi-vaar

supermarket　　पंसारी की दुकान
pan-saa-ree kee du-kaan

surprised　　आश्चर्य
ash-cha-rya

a b c d e f g h i j k l m n o p q r **s** t u v w x y z

sweater　　　　　　स्वेटर
sve-Tar

sweet　　　　　　मीठा
mee-Thaa

(to) swim　　　　तैरना
tair-naa

swimsuit　　　तैरने के कपड़े
tair-nay kay kap-Ray

swing　　　　　　झूला
jhuu-laa

table मेज़
mayz

tablecloth मेज़पोश
mez-posh

(to) talk बातचीत करना
baat-cheet kar-naa

tall लंबा
lam-baa

taxi टैक्सी
Taiksee

tea चाय
chai

a b c d e f g h i j k l m n o p q r s t u v w x y z

teacher अध्यापक
a-dhyaa-pak

teddy bear खिलौना भालू
khi-lau-naa bhaa-luu

telephone फ़ोन
fone

television टी. वी.
Tee. Vee.

10

ten दस
das

tennis टेनिस
Tay-nis

a b c d e f g h i j k l m n o p q r s t u v w x y z

tent तंबू
tam-buu

Thursday गुरुवार
guru-vaar

tiger बाघ
baagh

three तीन
teen

(to) tie बाँधना
baañdh-naa

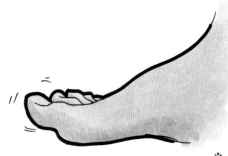

toe अँगुली
añ-gu-lee

a b c d e f g h i j k l m n o p q r s t u v w x y z

tomato टमाटर
Ta-maa-Tar

tooth दाँत
daañt

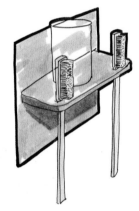

toothbrush दाँत का बश
daañt kaa brash

towel तौलिया
tau-li-yaa

toy खिलौना
khi-lau-naa

train रेलगाड़ी
rayl-gaa-Ree

a b c d e f g h i j k l m n o p q r s t u v w x y z

trash can कूड़ादान
kuu-Raa-daan

tree पेड़
payR

triangle त्रिकोण
tri-koN

truck ट्रक
Trak

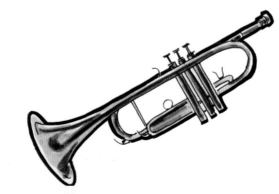

trumpet तुरही
tur-hee

a b c d e f g h i j k l m n o p q r s t u v w x y z

Tuesday मंगलवार
man-gal-vaar

tunnel सुरंग
su-rang

turtle हरा कछुआ
ha-raa ka-chu-aa

twins जुड़वाँ
juR-vaañ

2

two दो
do

a b c d e f g h i j k l m n o p q r s t u v w x y z

umbrella   छाता
Chaa-taa

underwear   अन्दर के कपड़े
an-dar kay kap-Ray

up   ऊपर
uu-par

upstairs   ऊपर
uu-par

a b c d e f g h i j k l m n o p q r s t **U** v w x y z

vacation
छुट्टी
Chu-T Tee

valley
घाटी
ghaa-Tee

vegetable
सब्ज़ी
sab-zee

violin
वायलिन
vaa-ya-lin

a b c d e f g h i j k l m n o p q r s t u **v** w x y z

wagon वैगन
vai-gan

waiter बैरा
bai-raa

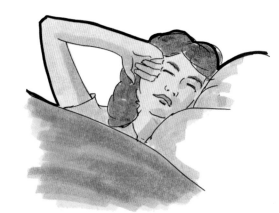

(to) wake up जागना
jaa-ga-naa

(to) walk पैदल जाना
pai-dal jaa-naa

wall दीवार
dee-vaar

wallet बटुआ
ba-Tu-aa

a b c d e f g h i j k l m n o p q r s t u v w x y z

(to) wash धोना
dho-naa

watch घड़ी
gha-Ree

(to) watch देखना
dekh-naa

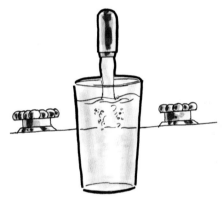

water पानी
paa-nee

waterfall झरना
jhar-naa

watermelon तरबूज
tar-buuz

Wednesday बुधवार
budh-vaar

wet गीला
gee-laa

whale ह्वेल
vhayl

wheel पहिया
pa-hi-yaa

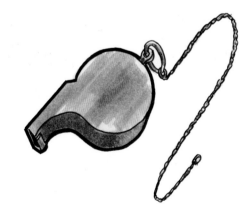

(to) whisper फुसफुसाना
phus-phu-saa-naa

whistle सीटी
see-Tee

a b c d e f g h i j k l m n o p q r s t u v **w** x y z

white सफेद़
sa-fayd

wind हवा
ha-vaa

window खिड़की
khiR-kee

wings पंख
pan-kha

winter जाड़ा
jaa-Raa

wolf भेड़िया
bhe-Ri-yaa

a b c d e f g h i j k l m n o p q r s t u v **W** x y z

woman औरत
au-rat

wood लकड़ी
la-ka-Ree

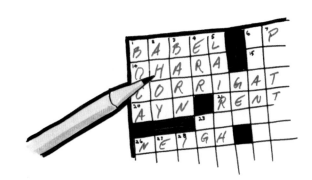

word शब्द
shabd

(to) work काम करना
kaam kar-naa

worm कीड़ा
kee-Raa

(to) write लिखना
liKh-naa

x-ray एकस रे
eks-ray

yard अहाता
a-haa-taa

(to) yawn जंभाई लेना
jam-bhaaee lay-naa

yellow पीला
pee-laa

yogurt दही
da-hee

young जवान
ja-vaan

a b c d e f g h i j k l m n o p q r s t u v w **x y z**

zebra ज़ेबरा
zay-ba-raa

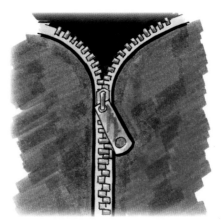

zipper ज़िप
zip

zoo चिड़ियाघर
chi-Ri-yaa-ghar

a b c d e f g h i j k l m n o p q r s t u v w x y **z**

mother माता जी
maa-taa-jee

father पिता जी
pitaa-jee

sister बहन
bahen

brother भाई
bhaaee

94

grandmother

(paternal)   दादी
daa-dee

(maternal)   नानी
naa-nee

grandfather

(paternal)   दादा
daa-daa

(maternal)   नाना
naa-naa

aunt

(father's sister)   बुआ
buaa

(mother's sister)   मौसी
mau-see

(father's brother's wife)   चाची
chaa-chee

(mother's brother's wife)   मामी
maa-mee

uncle

(father's elder brother)   ताऊ
taauu

(father's younger brother)   चाचा
caa-caa

(father's sister's husband)   फूफा
phuu-paa

(mother's brother)   मामा
maa-maa

(mother's sister's husband)   मौसा
mau-saa

WORD	TRANSLATION	PRONUNCIATION
Congratulations!	बधाई हो	ba-dhaaee ho
Excuse me.	माफ़ कीजिये	maaf kee-ji-yay
Good morning!	नमस्ते	na-mas-tay
How?	कैसे	kai-say
How are you?	आप कैसे हैं	aap kai-say haiń
How many?	कितने	kit-nay
How much?	कितना	kit-naa
I beg your pardon?	फिर से बोलिये	phir say bo-lı-yay
I know... (m.)	जानता हूँ	jaan-taa huuń
I know... (f.)	जानती हूँ	jaan-tee huuń
I don't know... (m.)	नहीं जानता	na-heeń jaan-taa
I don't know... (f.)	नहीं जानती	na-heeń jaan-tee
I like...	मुझे पसंद है	muj-hay ... pa-sand hai
I don't like...	मुझे नहीं पसंद है	muj-hay ... na-heeń pa-sand hai
I want to... (m.)	मैं ... चाहता हुँ	maiń ... chaah-taa huuń
I want to... (f.)	मैं ... चाहती हुँ	maiń ... chaah-tee huuń
I don't want to... (m.)	मैं ... नहीं चाहता	maiń na-heeń ... chaah-taa
I don't want to... (f.)	मैं ... नहीं चाहती	maiń na-heeń ... chaah-tee
I'm fine.	मैं ठीक हुँ	maiń theek huuń
I'm sorry.	माफ़ कीजिये	maaf kee-ji-yay
May I introduce you to...?	... से मिलिये	... say mi-li-yay
No.	नहीं	na-heeń
Please.	मेहरबानी	may-har-baa-nee
Pleased to meet you.	आप से मिल कर मुझे बहुत खुशी हुई	aap say mil kar muj-hay bahut khu-shee hu-ee
See you tomorrow!	कल मिलेंगे	kal mi-layń-gay
Thank you.	धन्यवाद	dha-nya-vaad
Thank you very much.	बहुत धन्यवाद	bahut dha-nya-vaad
Welcome!	स्वागतम	svaa-ga-tam
What?	क्या	kyaa
What is your name?	आप का नाम क्या है	aap kaa naam kyaa hai
My name is...	मेरा नाम ... है	may-raa naam ... hai
When?	कब	kab
Where?	कहाँ	ka-haań
Who?	कौन	kaun
Why?	क्यों	kyoń
Yes.	हाँ	haań
You're welcome.	कोई बात नहीं	koi baat na-heeń

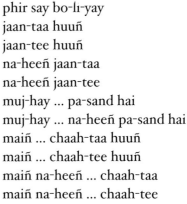

Honorifics & Pronouns

WORD	TRANSLATION	PRONUNCIATION
Mr.	श्री	shree
Miss	सुश्री	su-shree
Mrs.	श्रीमती	shree-ma-tee
I	मैं	maiñ
you (one person)	आप	aap
he	वह	voh
she	वह	voh
it	वह	voh
we	हम	ham
you (more than one person)	आप	aap
they	वे	vay

Time Expressions

A.M.	सुबह	su-bah
P.M.	शाम	shaam
today	आज	aaj
yesterday	कल	kal
tomorrow	कल	kal
midnight	आधी रात	aa-dhee raat
noon	दोपहर	do-pa-har
What time is it?	कितने बजे हैं	kit-nay ba-jay haiñ
The time is...	... बजे हैं	... ba-jay haiñ
0:00 (12:00 A.M.)	रात के बारह बजे हैं	raat kay baa-raa ba-jay haiñ
1:00	सुबह का एक बजा है	su-bah kaa ek ba-jaa hai
2:00	सुबह के दो बजे हैं	su-bah kay do ba-jay haiñ
3:00	सुबह के तीन बजे हैं	su-bah kay teen ba-jay haiñ
4:00	सुबह के चार बजे हैं	su-bah kay char ba-jay haiñ
5:00	सुबह के पाँच बजे हैं	su-bah kay paanch ba-jay haiñ
6:00	सुबह के छह बजे हैं	su-bah kay chay ba-jay haiñ
7:00	सुबह के सात बजे हैं	su-bah kay saat ba-jay haiñ
8:00	सुबह के आठ बजे हैं	su-bah kay aaTh ba-jay haiñ
9:00	सुबह के नौ बजे हैं	su-bah kay nau ba-jay haiñ

WORD	TRANSLATION	PRONUNCIATION
10:00	दिन के दस बजे हैं	din kay das ba-jay hain̄
11:00	दिन के ग्यारह बजे हैं	din kay gyaa-rah ba-jay hain̄
12:00	दिन के बारह बजे हैं	din kay baa-rah ba-jay hain̄
13:00 (1:00 P.M.)	दिन का एक बजा है	din kaa ek ba-jaa hai
14:00 (2:00 P.M.)	दिन के दो बजे हैं	din kay do ba-jay hain̄
15:00 (3:00 P.M.)	दिन के तीन बजे हैं	din kay teen ba-jay hain̄
16:00 (4:00 P.M.)	दिन के चार बजे हैं	din kay chaar ba-jay hain̄
17:00 (5:00 P.M.)	शाम के पाँच बजे हैं	shaam kay paan̄ch ba-jay hain̄
18:00 (6:00 P.M.)	शाम के छह बजे हैं	shaam kay chay ba-jay hain̄
19:00 (7:00 P.M.)	शाम के सात बजे हैं	shaam kay saat ba-jay hain̄
20:00 (8:00 P.M.)	रात के आठ बजे हैं	raat kay aaTh ba-jay hain̄
21:00 (9:00 P.M.)	रात के नौ बजे हैं	raat kay nau ba-jay hain̄
22:00 (10:00 P.M.)	रात के दस बजे हैं	raat kay das ba-jay hain̄
23:00 (11:00 P.M.)	रात के ग्यारह बजे हैं	raat kay gyaa-rah ba-jay hain̄
a quarter after	सवा ... बजे हैं	sa-vaa ... ba-jay hain̄
half past six	साढ़े ... बजे हैं	saa-Rhay ... ba-jay hain̄
three quarters after	पौने ... बजे हैं	pau-nay ... ba-jay hain
a quarter 'til	पौने ... बजे हैं	pau-nay ... ba-jay hain̄

Months

January	जनवरी	jan-va-ree
February	फ़रवरी	far-va-ree
March	मार्च	maarch
April	अप्रैल	a-prail
May	मई	maee
June	जून	juun
July	जुलाई	ju-laaee
August	अगस्त	a-gast
September	सितम्बर	si-tam-bar
October	अक्तूबर	ak-tuu-bar
November	नवम्बर	na-vam-bar
December	दिसम्बर	di-sam-bar

WORD	TRANSLATION	PRONUNCIATION
eleven (11)	ग्यारह	gyaa-rah
twelve (12)	बारह	baa-rah
thirteen (13)	तेरह	tay-rah
fourteen (14)	चौदह	cau-dah
fifteen (15)	पंद्रह	pan-drah
sixteen (16)	सोलह	so-lah
seventeen (17)	सत्रह	sa-trah
eighteen (18)	अठारह	a-Thaa-rah
nineteen (19)	उन्नीस	unnees
twenty (20)	बीस	bees
twenty-one (21)	इक्कीस	ikkees
twenty-two (22)	बाईस	baais
twenty-three (23)	तेईस	tay-ees
twenty-four (24)	चौबीस	cau-bees
twenty-five (25)	पच्चीस	pacchees
twenty-six (26)	छब्बीस	chabbees
twenty-seven (27)	सत्ताईस	sattaaees
twenty-eight (28)	अट्ठाईस	aTThaaees
twenty-nine (29)	उनतीस	un-tees
thirty (30)	तीस	tees
forty (40)	चालीस	chaa-lees
fifty (50)	पचास	pa-chaas
sixty (60)	साठ	saaTh
seventy (70)	सत्तर	sattar
eighty (80)	अस्सी	assee
ninety (90)	नब्बे	nabbay
one hundred (100)	सौ	sau
one thousand (1000)	हज़ार	ha-zaar
ten thousand (10,000)	दस हज़ार	das ha-zaar
hundred thousand (100,000)	एक लाख	ek laakh
one million (1,000,000)	दस लाख	das laakh
one billion (1,000,000,000)	एक अरब	ek a-rab
one trillion (1,000,000,000,000)	एक लाख करोड़	ek laakh karoR

अ	
अक्तूबर	October
अँगुली	finger
अँगूठी	ring
अंगूर	grapes
अण्डा	egg
अन्दर के कपड़े	underwear
अगस्त	August
अट्ठाईस	twenty-eight (28)
अठारह	eighteen (18)
अध्यापक	teacher
अप्रैल	April
अलमारी	cabinet, closet
अस्पताल	hospital
अस्पताल गाड़ी	ambulance
अस्सी	eighty (80)
अहाता	yard

आ	
आँख	eye
आइसक्रीम	ice cream
आकाश	sky
आग	fire
आग बुझाने वाला	firefighter
आज	today
आठ	eight
आडू	peach
आदमी	man
आधी रात	midnight
आप	you
आप का नाम क्या है	What is your name?
आप कैसे हैं	How are you?
आप से मिल कर मुझे बहुत खुशी हुई	Pleased to meet you.
आयत	rectangle
आलू	potato
आश्चर्य	surprised

इ	
इक्कीस	twenty-one (21)
इन्द्रधनुष	rainbow
इमारत	building
इल्ली	caterpillar

उ	
उकाब	eagle
उड़ना	(to) fly
उदास	sad
उनतीस	twenty-nine (29)
उन्नीस	nineteen (19)
उपहार	gift

ऊ	
ऊँट	camel
ऊपर	up, upstairs

ए	
एक	one
एक अरब	one billion (1,000,000,000)
एक लाख	hundred thousand (100,000)
एक लाख करोड़	one trillion (1,000,000,000,000)
एकस रे	x-ray

औ	
औरत	woman

क	
कंगन	bracelet
कंगारू	kangaroo
कंघी	comb
कंधा	shoulder
कंबल	blanket
कटोरा	bowl
कब	When?
कमीज़	shirt
कंप्यूटर	computer
कद्दू	pumpkin
क़दम	steps
कल	tomorrow, yesterday
कल मिलेंगे	See you tomorrow!
क़लम	pen
कहाँ	Where?
काँटा	fork
काग़ज़	paper

कान	ear
काम करना	(to) work
काला	black
काली मिर्च	pepper
कितना	How much?
कितने	How many?
कितने बजे हैं	What time is it?
किताब	book
किला	castle
कीड़ा	worm
कील	nail
कूड़ादान	trash can
कुत्ता	dog
कुम्हड़ा	squash
कुर्सी	chair
कूदना	(to) jump
केक	cake
केला	banana
कैंची	scissors
कैमरा	camera
कैलेंडर	calendar
कैसे	How?
कोई बात नहीं	You're welcome.
कोट	coat
कौन	Who?
कौफ़ी	coffee
क्या	What?
क्यों	Why?

ख

खटोला	crib
खट्टा	sour
खड़ा होना	(to) stand
ख़रगोश	rabbit
खरीदना	(to) buy
खाना	(to) eat
ख़ाली	empty
खिड़की	window
खिलाना	(to) feed
खिलौना	toy
खिलौना भालू	teddy bear
खींचना	(to) pull
खुश	happy

खेल	game
खेलना	(to) play
खोलना	(to) open

ग

गंदा	dirty
गधा	donkey
गरम	hot
गरमी	summer
गले लगाना	(to) hug
गाँठ	knot
गाजर	carrot
गाड़ी	car
गाड़ी स्थान	parking lot
गाना	(to) sing
गाल	cheek
गॉल्फ़	golf
गिटार	guitar
गिलहरी	squirrel
गीला	wet
गुड़िया	doll
गुफ़ा	cave
गुब्बारा	balloon
गुरुवार	Thursday
गुलाब	rose
गुलाबी	pink
गुसलखाना	bathroom
गेंद	ball
गोला	circle
ग्यारह	eleven (11)
ग्लास	glass
ग्लोब	globe
ग्रह	planet

घ

घंटा	bell
घड़ी	clock, watch
घुटना	knee
घाघरा	skirt
घाटी	valley
घोंसला	nest
घोड़ा	horse

च	
चन्द्र	moon
चट्टान	rock
चढ़ना	(to) climb
चप्पल	sandal
चम्मच	spoon
चलती सीढ़ी	escalator
चश्मा	eyeglasses
चाकू	knife
चाचा	uncle (father's younger brother)
चाची	aunt (father's brother's wife)
चाबी	key
चाय	tea
चार	four
चावल	rice
चालीस	forty (40)
चिक्	blinds
चिड़िया	bird
चिड़ियाघर	zoo
चित्रांकनी	crayon
चिल्लाना	(to) shout
चींटी	ant
चीनी	sugar
चील	kite
चुम्मा	kiss
चुहिया	mouse
चेरी	cherry
चेहरा	face
चौकोर	square
चौदह	fourteen (14)
चौबीस	twenty-four (24)
छ	
छत	ceiling, roof
छब्बीस	twenty-six (26)
छह	six
छाता	umbrella
छिपकली	lizard
छिपाना	(to) hide
छींकना	(to) sneeze

छुट्टी	vacation
छोटा	short, small
ज	
जंगल	jungle
जंभाई	(to) yawn
जनवरी	January
जन्मदिन	birthday
जवान	young
जाकेट	jackct
जागना	(to) wake up
जाड़ा	winter
जानता हूँ	I know... (m.)
जानती हूँ	I know... (f.)
ज़िप	zipper
जिराफ़	giraffe
जुड़वाँ	twins
जुलाई	July
जूता	shoe
जून	June
जूते का फ़ीता	shoelaces
जेब	pocket
जेबरा	zebra
जैम	jam
झ	
झण्डा	flag
झरना	waterfall
झाड़ू	broom
झूला	swing
झूमाझूमी	seesaw
ट	
टमाटर	tomato
टाँग	leg
टापू	island
टॉर्च	flashlight
टिड्डा	grasshopper
टी. वी.	television
टेनिस	tennis
टैक्सी	taxi
टोकरी	basket
टोपी	hat
ट्रक	truck

ठ

ठण्डा	cold

ड

डरा हुआ	afraid
डाइनसॉर	dinosaur
डाक घर	post office
डाकिया	mail carrier
डॉक्टर	doctor
डॉलफ़िन	dolphin
डिब्बा	box
डेस्क	desk
ड्रैगन	dragon
ड्रैस	dress

ढ

ढोना	(to) carry
ढोल	drum

त

तंबू	tent
तकिया	pillow
तरबूज़	watermelon
ताऊ	uncle (father's elder brother)
तारा	star
तितली	butterfly
तीन	three
तीस	thirty (30)
तुरही	trumpet
तेईस	twenty-three (23)
तेज़	loud
तेरह	thirteen (13)
तैरना	(to) swim
तैरने के कपड़े	swimsuit
तोता	parrot
तौलिया	towel
त्रिकोण	triangle

द

दमकल	fire engine
दरवाज़ा	door
दराज़	drawer
दरियाई घोड़ा	hippopotamus
दरी	carpet
दर्पण	mirror
दवा	medicine
दस	ten
दस लाख	one million (1,000,000)
दस हज़ार	ten thousand (10,000)
दस्ताना	mitten
दही	yogurt
दाँत	tooth
दाँत का ब्रश	toothbrush
दादा	grandfather (paternal)
दादी	grandmother (paternal)
दिन का खाना	lunch
दिन का एक बजा है	13:00 (1:00 P.M.)
दिन के ग्यारह बजे हैं	11:00
दिन के चार बजे हैं	16:00 (4:00 P.M.)
दिन के तीन बजे हैं	15:00 (3:00 P.M.)
दिन के दस बजे हैं	10:00
दिन के दो बजे हैं	14:00 (2:00 P.M.)
दिन के बारह बजे हैं	12:00
दिल	heart
दिसम्बर	December
दीवार	wall
दुपट्टा	scarf
दूध	milk
दूरबीन	binoculars
देखना	(to) watch
देना	(to) give
दो	two
दोपहर	noon
दोस्त	friend
दौड़ना	(to) run

ध

धन्यवाद	Thank you.
धुआँ	smoke
धोना	(to) wash

न

नक्शा	map
नकाब	mask
नदी	river
नब्बे	ninety (90)
नमक	salt

नमस्ते	Good morning! Good-bye. Hello.	पहेली	jigsaw puzzle
नवम्बर	November	पाँच	five
नर्स	nurse	पाइ	pie
नहीं	No.	पार्क	park
नहीं जानता	I don't know... (m.)	पाजामा	pajamas
नहीं जानती	I don't know... (f.)	पानी	water
नाचना	(to) dance	पार्टी	party
नाना	grandfather (maternal)	पिता जी	father
नानी	grandmother (maternal)	पियानो	piano
नाभि	bellybutton	पिल्ला	puppy
नाम	name	पीना	(to) drink
नारंगी	orange [color]	पीपा	barrel
नाराज़	angry	पीला	yellow
नाव	boat	पुतली	puppet
नाशपाती	pear	पुराना	old
नाश्ता	breakfast	पुल	bridge
नीचे	downstairs	पुलिस	police officer
नीचे	down	पुस्तकालय	library
नीबू	lemon	पूर्ण	full
नीला	blue	पेंचकश	screwdriver
नैपकिन	napkin	पेंसिल	pencil
नौ	nine	पेंट	paint
प		पेट	stomach
		पेटी	belt, chest
पंख	wings	पेट्रोल	gasoline
पंखा	fan	पेड़	tree
पंद्रह	fifteen (15)	पैदल जाना	(to) walk
पंसारी की दुकान	supermarket	पैर	foot
पकाना	(to) cook	पैर की अँगुली	toe
पचास	fifty (50)	पैसा	money
पच्चीस	twenty-five (25)	पोस्ट बॉक्स	mailbox
पड़ोस	neighborhood	पौने ... बजे हैं	a quarter 'til
पढ़ना	(to) read	पौने ... बजे हैं	three quarters after
पतझड़	autumn	प्लेट	plate
पतलून	pants	प्राम	stroller
पत्ता	leaf	**फ**	
पनीर	cheese		
पर	feather	फ़रवरी	February
परदा	curtain	इ	fruit
परिवार	family	फ़र्श	floor
पर्स	purse	फ़व्वारा	fountain
पहाड़	mountain	फिर से बोलिये	I beg your pardon?
पहिया	wheel	फुटपाथ	sidewalk
		फुटबाल	soccer

फुसफुसाना	(to) whisper
फ़ूफ़ा	uncle (father's sister's husband)
फूल	flower
फ़ोटो	photograph
फ़ोन	telephone
फ़्लैट	apartment
फ्रिज़	refrigerator
ब	
बन्द करना	(to) close
बन्दर	monkey
बच्चा	baby, child
... बजे हैं	The time is...
बटुआ	wallet
बड़ा	big
बतख़	duck
बधाई हो	Congratulations!
बर्फ़	ice cube, snow
बर्फ़ गाड़ी	sled
बर्फ़ पर स्केटिंग करना	ice-skating
बस	bus
बहन	sister
बहुत धन्यवाद	Thank you very much.
बाँधना	(to) tie
बाँह	arm
बाईस	twenty-two (22)
बाग़	garden
बाघ	tiger
बाड़	fence
बातचीत करना	(to) talk
बादल	cloud
बाँसुरी	flute
बारह	twelve (12)
बारिश	rain
बाल	hair
बाल्टी	bucket
बालियाँ	earring
बिलौटा	kitten
बिल्ली	cat
बिस्कुट	cracker
बिस्तर	bed
बीमार	sick
बीर बहुटा	ladybug
बीस	twenty (20)

बुआ	aunt (father's sister)
बुधवार	Wednesday
बेंच	bench
बेसबॉल	baseball
बैंक	bank
बैंगनी	purple
बैठक	living room
बैठना	(to) sit
बैट	bat
बैरा	waiter
बोतल	bottle
ब्लॉक्स	blocks
ब्रश	brush
भ	
भट्टी	oven
भाई	brother
भालू	bear
भूमिगत रेलवे	subway
भूरा	brown
भेड़	sheep
भेड़िया	wolf
भांरा	beetle
भौंह	eyebrow
म	
मंगलवार	Tuesday
मई	May
मकड़ी	spider
मकान	house
मक्का	corn
मक्खन	butter
मगर	crocodile
मछली	fish
मज़दूर	construction worker
मधुमक्खी	bee
मर्तबान	jar
महासागर	ocean
माता जी	mother
माफ़ कीजिये	I'm sorry.
माफ़ कीजिये	Excuse me.
मामा	uncle (mother's brother)
मामी	aunt (mother's brother's wife)
मार्च	March

Hindi	English
मिठाई	candy, dessert
मीठा	sweet
मीठा बिस्कुट	cookie
मुँह	mouth
मुझे पसंद है	I like...
मुझे नहीं पसंद है	I don't like...
मुरगा	rooster
मुर्गी	chicken
मुस्कराहट	smile
मेंढक	frog
मेज़	table
मेज़पोश	tablecloth
मेन्यू	menu
मेमना	lamb
मेरा नाम ... है	My name is...
मेहरबानी	Please.
मैं	I
मैं ... चाहता हुँ	I want to... (m.)
मैं ... चाहती हुँ	I want to... (f.)
मैं ठीक हुँ	I'm fine.
मैं ... नहीं चाहता	I don't want to... (m.)
मैं ... नहीं चाहती	I don't want to... (f.)
मोज़ा	sock
मोमबत्ती	candle
मौसा	uncle (mother's sister's husband)
मौसी	aunt (mother's sister)

र

रविवार	Sunday
रस	juice
रसोईघर	kitchen
रसोइया	chef
राजमार्ग	highway
राजा	king
रात	night
रात का खाना	dinner
रात के आठ बजे हैं	20:00 (8:00 P.M.)
रात के ग्यारह बजे हैं	23:00 (11:00 P.M.)
रात के दस बजे हैं	22:00 (10:00 P.M.)
रात के नौ बजे हैं	21:00 (9:00 P.M.)
रात के बारह बजे हैं	0:00 (12:00 A.M.)
रानी	queen
रेंगना	(to) crawl
रेगिस्तान	desert
रेडियो	radio

Hindi	English
रेलगाड़ी	train
रेस्तराँ	restaurant
रोटी	bread
रोना	(to) cry

ल

लंबा	tall
लकड़ी	wood
लड़का	boy
लड़की	girl
लाल	red
लिखना	(to) write
लिफ़ाफ़ा	envelope
लिफ़्ट	elevator
लैंप	lamp
लोग	people
लोमड़ी	fox

व

वन	forest
वर्णमाला	alphabet
वसंत	spring
वह	he, it, she
वायलिन	violin
विदूषक	clown
विद्यालय	school
वे	they
वैगन	wagon
व्यायाम	gymnastics
वृत्त	circle

श

शनिवार	Saturday
शब्द	word
शहर	city
शान्त	quiet
शाम	evening, P.M.
शाम के पाँच बजे हैं	17:00 (5:00 P.M.)
शाम के छह बजे हैं	18:00 (6:00 P.M.)
शाम के सात बजे हैं	19:00 (7:00 P.M.)
शुक्रवार	Friday
शुभ रात्रि	Good night.
शोरबा	soup
श्री	Mr.
श्रीमती	Mrs.

स

संग्रहालय	museum
सन्तरा	orange [fruit]
सड़क	road, street
सत्तर	seventy (70)
सत्ताईस	twenty-seven (27)
सत्रह	seventeen (17)
सफ़ेद	white
सब्ज़ी	vegetable
समाचारपत्र	newspaper
समुद्र तट	beach
समुद्री झींगा	lobster
सरकस	circus
स्लाइड	slide
सलाद	salad
सवारी करना	(to) ride
सवा ... बजे हैं	a quarter after
सवेरा	morning
साँप	snake
साइकिल	bicycle
साठ	sixty (60)
साढ़े ... बजे हैं	half past
सात	seven
साबुन	soap
सिंह	lion
सितम्बर	September
सिनेमा	movie theater
सिर	head
सीटी	whistle
सीढ़ी	ladder
सीप	shell
सुबह	A.M.
सुबह का एक बजा है	1:00
सुबह के आठ बजे हैं	8:00
सुबह के चार बजे हैं	4:00
सुबह के छह बजे हैं	6:00
सुबह के तीन बजे हैं	3:00
सुबह के दो बजे हैं	2:00
सुबह के नौ बजे हैं	9:00
सुबह के पाँच बजे हैं	5:00
सुबह के सात बजे हैं	7:00

सुरंग	tunnel
सुश्री	Miss
सूअर	pig
सूटकेस	suitcase
सूर्य	sun
... से मिलिये	May I introduce you to...?
सेब	apple
सेम	beans
सैंडविच	sandwich
सैक्सोफ़ोन	saxophone
सोना	(to) sleep
सोने का कमरा	bedroom
सोफ़ा	sofa
सोमव	Monday
सोलह	sixteen (16)
सौ	one hundred (100)
स्कीइंग करना	skiing
स्ट्राबेरी	strawberry
स्नान का टब	bathtub
स्वागतम	Welcome!
स्वेटर	sweater

ह

हँडिया	pot
हँसना	(to) laugh
हज़ार	one thousand (1000)
हथौड़ा	hammer
हम	we
हरा	green
हरा कछुआ	turtle
हवा	wind
हवाई जहाज़	airplane
हाँ	Yes.
हाँगर	shark
हाथ	hand
हार	necklace
हाथी	elephant
हिरन	deer
हीरा	diamond
हेलिकाप्टर	helicopter
हौज़	sink
हेल	whale

Hindi Dictionary & Phrasebook

Hindi-English
English-Hindi

Hindi is one of the word's most widely spoken languages and one of the official languages of India. This guide provides students, travelers, and businesspeople with an essential resource for communication.

- Over 3,400 total dictionary entries
- Basic Hindi grammar and pronunciation
- All Hindi words featured in both Devanagari script and romanized form
- Includes cultural notes and advice

3,400 entries • 286 pages • 3 3/4 x 7 1/2 • ISBN 0-7818-0983-5 • $12.95pb • (488)

India: An Illustrated History

By Prem Kishore & Anuradha Kishore Ganpati

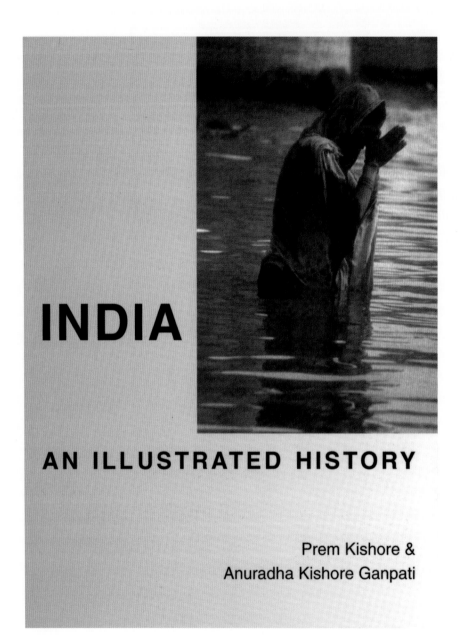

This succinct volume recounts 45,000 years of Indian history, from the earliest settlements of the Indus Valley through the twentieth-century struggle against British imperial rule. It concludes with a discussion of the challenges facing the country today. Sections on dress, regional cuisine, and cultural traditions bring the various aspects of this diverse nation to life.

234 pages • 5 x 7 • 50 photos/illus./maps • $14.95 paperback • 0-7818-0944-4 • (424)

Hindi Standard Dictionary

By Joseph W. Raker and Rama Shankar Shukla

Hindi-English
English-Hindi

- Over 30,000 entries
- Hindi words featured in Devanagari script and roman transliteration
- Includes a separate glossary of government and official terms
- Features a guide to pronunciation and transliteration
- Ideal for students and scholars

30,000 entries • 848 pages • 5 1/2 x 8 1/2 • $27.50pb • 0-7818-0470-1 • (559)

Available in 6 additional languages!

Hippocrene Bengali Children's Picture Dictionary
English-Bengali/Bengali-English
625 entries • 104 pages • 8 1/2 x 11 • $14.95pb • 0-7818-1128-7 • (324)

Hippocrene Brazilian Portuguese Children's Picture Dictionary
English-Brazilian Portuguese/Brazilian Portuguese-English
625 entries • 104 pages • 8 1/2 x 11 • $14.95pb • 0-7818-1131-7 • (318)

Hippocrene Korean Children's Picture Dictionary
English-Korean/Korean-English
625 entries • 104 pages • 8 1/2 x 11 • $14.95pb • 0-7818-1132-5 • (323)

Hippocrene Polish Children's Picture Dictionary
English-Polish/Polish-English
625 entries • 104 pages • 8 1/2 x 11 • $14.95pb • 0-7818-1127-9 • (358)

Hippocrene Spanish Children's Picture Dictionary
English-Spanish/Spanish-English
625 entries • 104 pages • 8 1/2 x 11 • $14.95pb • 0-7818-1130-9 • (345)

Hippocrene Vietnamese Children's Picture Dictionary
English-Vietnamese/Vietnamese-English
625 entries • 104 pages • 8 1/2 x 11 • $14.95pb • 0-7818-1133-3 • (347)

Prices subject to change without prior notice. To order **Hippocrene Books**, contact your local bookstore, call (718) 454-2366, visit www.hippocrenebooks.com, or write to: Hippocrene Books, 171 Madison Avenue, New York, NY 10016. Please enclose check or money order adding $5.00 shipping (UPS) for the first book and $.50 for each additional title.